HOW TO TEXT A GIRL (GODLY TEXTING)

DATE AND SEX GUARANTEED

BASED ZEUS

Copyright © 2022 Based Zeus

All rights reserved.

ISBN: **9798355233556**

DEDICATION

This book is dedicated to all those men who don't know how text a girl and keep the conversation going, what to do if the girl doesn't respond to your text and how create sexual tension over text.

HOW TO TEXT A GIRL (GODLY TEXTING)

CHAPTER 1

The Based Mindset

How to Signal your Confidence via Text

The Power of texting

CHAPTER 2

What to do when you get her number

The Best Openers

How to use Emojis to Build Sexual Tension

Text, Tease, and Takeoff: In-Depth

How to Tease a Girl over Text

How to flirt like a God

CHAPTER 3

What to do when she doesn't reply

How to keep a conversation going

The Pull away: In-Depth

How to know if she likes you over Text

How to make her text you first

The Best way to ask her to Hangout

A final message from the God

CHAPTER 1

The Based Mindset

Oh fuck yeah baby. You just did it. You fucking did it! Congratulations!

You just proved that you're an ACTION TAKER who is ready to take your texting game to the next level and start fucking bitches left and right. Now you got full access inside the God's mind and TRUST me, your text game, and more importantly, your self-perception and life with girls is gonna change.

But first, in order to REALLY be able to execute on the tips and advice I'm gonna be giving you, the first and most fundamental thing you need to be willing to change is your mindset.

Once your mindset changes, the texting game will change with it. That's why your mindset is

THE most important thing to focus on, since it will change your whole approach to this.

Because once you master what I call the Based Mindset, the texting tips will be ingrained in you, and godly game will begin to flow naturally.

First and foremost, fuck everything you've learned in the past and everything you THINK works with girls. I want you to go into this totally open-minded and willing to take risks with the girls you're gonna be going after. And I'm nottalking about some hashtag Me Too risks, FUCK

THAT.

HOW TO TEXT A GIRL (GODLY TEXTING)

You have to be ready to step out of your comfort zone and do the shit I'm telling you, because it WILL work. Not only will it work, but it will change your mindset so that you're must understand that at first your new approach might fail, but as you'll practice, you'll learn and constantly willing to take risks and try new things. If you really want to make some progress, you get even a deeper understanding of what I'm trying to say and it will help you in the long run.

Second, I want you to destroy your fear and realize that this shit is not that serious. Honestly, like this shit is NOT that serious. You're a young guy who's texting a girl you're into, what's the worst case scenario if you fuck up? You miss out on getting one girl? Newsflash! There's like 3 billion more where that came from. You need to understand that the girl that's so special and important to you right now, will most likely be totally irrelevant 6 months from now and EVEN MORE irrelevant 6 years from now. And now I know someone is gonna say, "But Zeus what if she's the one" well then in that case, that's only like 1% of the time, so for the time being, it's just safer to assume the girl you're talking to ISN'T the one you'll likely end up marrying. Besides, if she WAS the one, then she'd be into you anyways and it wouldn't be so complicated.

It's not like you can't change the way you perceive her later on if she turns out to be really special. All these girls seem special to you only because you aren't that experienced, but once you start dating around and getting to know more people, you will see that all these characteristics that seem "special" about the girl you're talking to are actually pretty common.

So with this knowledge in mind, all fear should be erased from your mind and you should feel empowered knowing that each individual girl you meet isn't THAT important, and that life will go on, regardless if you smash that girl or not.

The third thing about the Based Mindset that will separate you from

99% of the population is that we TAKE ACTION. We don't spend months and years planning and perfecting every little thing, FUCK THAT. We just do and figure shit out on the go. We think of something, come up with a quick game plan, and just start executing because regardless of how you THINK something is gonna work out, it's most likely gonna change and turn out differently anyways, so you need to be ready to welcome those changes and be ready to adapt to them. THE most important thing, is that you switch to an action mindset, instead of a passive one. Fourth, I'd like you to think quantity, not so much quality when you're first learning and applying these techniques. Be willing to practice these on girls you're not that into, or girls you think are ugly as fuck, because the most important thing I want you to take away from all of this is learning to actually apply what I'm teaching you and get an understanding for yourself in the field.

By the end of this course, you should have practiced your texting game with at least 50 girls and that's when it'll be time to get the 9s and 10s, or the girls you REALLY care about, because you'll be ready and at that point texting girls will be a natural built-in instinct for you.

So I need you to be ready to play the numbers game, and more importantly, be ready to take rejection and feed off of it.

Lastly, I want your number one priority to be LEARNING. I need your mind to shift from being focused on getting some pussy, to being focused on becoming the best you can be with this skill.

Your focus needs to be on making progress, talking to more girls, exercising your texting skills, and more importantly, learning to become better and better, EACH and EVERY day.

In summary:

- Fuck everything you learned in the past. Be open minded

- Be fearless. No girl is that serious, or important.

- Be ready to take action.

- Think quantity, and be ready to master your skills on tons of girls.

- And focus on learning.

If you think you're ready to do this, then I'm gonna shut up and get right down to business because, it's only up from here. Let's fucking go.

How to Signal Your Confidence via Text

Confidence is the number one most important trait for you to have. Being confident will impact and more importantly, change every aspect of your life for the better. No joke. I cannot stress this enough. Confidence is the force multiplier for the good life and it's one of the most important aspects of the Based mindset. No matter what you try to do, whether or not you will be successful starts with you being confident. It's the first step to everything and not being confident in what you do will kill your efficiency, because if you're not confident you start overthinking, act emotionally and take less risk, which as I said in the previous videos is one of the key things for growth.

Confidence will also dramatically simplify the texting game for you. Confidence will allow you to send texts without overthinking every little aspect of the message you're sending AND it'll allow you to send text messages that make the girl actually want to hangout with you, because you will stand out and actually seem like a guy she could have fun with.

Becoming an uber-confident badass who doesn't second guess himself and doesn't give a flying fuck what anyone else thinks is something that requires work. A lot of it.

BUT luckily for you, I'm gonna teach you a few simple ways to signal this confidence over text in order to make her think you actually are confident AND increase her level of attraction for you.

#1 Use confident and affirmative language

The easiest way to signal your confidence to her over text is to use confident and affirmative language. For example, instead of saying something like "Do you wanna hangout?" you would say "Let's hangout" or "We should hangout" instead. Framing it as a question puts her in a position of authority and puts you in a position wherein you're seeking authority.

This is why it's better to frame it as a statement. It's also EVEN better if you offer an activity in there as well because it comes off as even more confident since you're assuming she's gonna say yes.

Other confident phrases and words to use are things like "I am", "I will" "We will", and so on.

You get the idea. And when you're not sure what the confident or slick thing to say is, just think to yourself what Based Muthafuckin Zeus say, and just say would fuck it and say that. Take the risk and TRUST ME you'll reap the benefits because so many guys pussyfoot about their intentions instead of being straight up. So when you do act straight up, the girl will love it and you'll establish that flirty vibe via text message, instantly.

#2 Assume attraction.

A really easy way to signal your confidence is to assume she's already into you and act like it in your conversations. Treat her like she's the one that's into you and like she has to work for you.

This will change up the dynamic and position you as the confident one that she needs to chase instead of you chasing her.

Sending the girl messages that position you above her are another really easy way to signal your confidence to her through text and make her think you're a confident badass that she

NEEDS to be with. This is a really important skill you need to practice and the best way to do it is to actually be confident. And an easy way to be confident over text is to actually get good at texting and practice it a shit ton so it becomes a routine thing, because to be honest, you will quickly realize that most conversations follow the same patterns.

#3 Use what I call 'Confident Text Game'

Practice your confident tone over text with every girl you talk to and test which phrases and tones work best for you, because different guys feel natural doing different things. That's why I'm not trying to make you remember specific phrases or texts you should send to girls. Instead, I'm trying to make you understand how these social dynamics work and help you find a way to give off the necessary vibes to succeed while still being yourself. You'll easily find a good cadence after you talk to enough girls.

This is what "Confident Text Game" is all about. Talking to so many girls, and being so used to texting, that your game starts to flow naturally. Practice with girls you match with on Tinder and don't be afraid to practice on ugly girls like I've mentioned before. This is a pivotal aspect to being able to text girls in a way that will make them like you so you DEFINITELY need to practice confidence signaling because it'll easily make you stand out from all the other guys.

Like I said in the beginning, focusing on making progress with this skill, and learning to do it so well that it just becomes second nature. I've practiced this shit so much and I'm so confident already that confident text messages flow out of me like a fucking pipe. You WILL get to this level. Everyone can. You just need to practice it. A LOT. I'm not gonna bullshit you and say that I'll magically get you to that level, fuck that, you need to put that work in but as long as you're willing to do it then you should have no problem doing that, but remember that it takes discipline and you will have to go through a lot of failure before you get there.

An easy way to get there is to practice and see which affirmative phrases work best for you.

In my later videos, I breakdown more specific tools and tactics for you to practice, so once you start practicing them on every girl you talk to, you'll notice IMMEDIATE improvements in your text game, and you'll immediately start getting more responses, and more dates.

In summary:

• Use confident and affirmative language

• When in doubt, say what I would say

• Assume attraction aka assume she's already into you

• Hone your Confident Text Game by practicing on ugly girls on Tinder

• And find the natural confident rhythm that works best for you because once you do, your text game will become so natural that you'll be getting girls through text, effortlessly.

Keeping in mind these key principles when you text a girl are what's gonna lay the foundation of your text game, and make the rest of the tips come naturally to you. And soon, you're gonna get so godly at texting, that you're gonna start coming up with YOUR OWN unique tricks and tactics.

And that brings me to your homework for today's video.

Homework: Go and practice affirmative phrases on 3 girls you talk to. If you're not currently talking to girls, then go on Tinder and find some to practice on. Remember, the goal here is to train yourself to always use affirmative and confident language, so you don't end up looking like a bitch when texting the girl you like.

That's all for today.

You already proved that you're willing to invest in yourself and become the god-like version of yourself by signing up for this course and getting this far. So let's keep fucking killing it baby.

The Power of Texting

Texting is fucking awesome. It's also a really new addition to the dating game. No joke, texting has made it so much easier for me to get pussy in the last 10 years, but for thousands of years

I had to get pussy the old fashioned way, no texting involved.

In fact, in order for you to even be born, your grandpa had to get pussy WITHOUT texting.

Just imagine that shit for a second, the only way you can get pussy is by physically going up and talking to every single girl you like. And the only way to communicate with them is to do so in person.

Now that texting is involved, it's made dating awesome because now you can keep constant contact with a girl and keep the momentum of your interactions going even while you're not in person. The best thing is that you can do it while you're just going about your day and you don't actually have to invest any real amount of time into it. That's why even if you have failures, you aren't really losing anything, so getting girls over text is a situation where you can't lose. But texting has also made dating fucking terrible.

SO many guys fuck up the texting because they don't understand what the real power of texting is. In fact, so many guys are so bad at texting that when you approach a girl for the first time, she usually assumes that you are just another boring guy who has nothing interesting to say.

That's why it's important to catch her attention and make yourself stand out from the start and break this negative prejudice.

Texting is a tool to get you more dates. Literally burn this sentence in your mind and remember this every time you're texting a girl.

When talking to a girl over text, you should be thinking to yourself, "How does this get me closer to hanging out with her".

If it's not getting you closer to a date, then it's a waste of time. There is one exception to this rule though, if you're using texting to flirt with a girl and maintain momentum, then that's acceptable because that momentum you're building is just to get her to want to hangout with you again.

If you meet a girl briefly in person, or you get her number from Instagram or Tinder or some other shit like that, then the other purpose of texting is to establish rapport with her and show her that you're not a fucking weirdo.

Texting will easily ease her potential worries that you might kidnap her in and sell her organs out of a van. But if you keep texting a girl for weeks and never ask her out to hang out with you, it's pointless. Not only are you wasting your time, but you are also making the girl less interested, because you are treating her as a friend, instead of a potential partner, and you are making yourself look like someone who isn't an action-taker. Whenever I text girls, it never takes me more than anywhere between one day and maximum two weeks of texting before I ask them out. And if it takes me two weeks, it's only because I was busy and couldn't do it sooner.

The point is, you should always aim for an actual meeting and talk in person instead of wasting time on endless discussion over text.

When it comes to gaining a girl's trust, Snapchat is another really easy way to do it, because it'll prove to her that you're not a 40 year old guy who's gonna roofie her and steal her organs in a beat-up rusty van. Again, that's not the vibe you wanna go for here. And if you drive a van, then you might wanna trade that shit in for like a punch buggy or something really nonthreatening

haha.

Appearing non-threatening is a really important thing to remember, because it's a vital part when it comes to texting any new girl. Girls are far more cautious and paranoid about guys being potentially dangerous, because if a girl is hot, then there's a ton of guys who are always drooling over and fantasizing about her, which increases her chances of getting kidnapped and thrown into a van. Okay okay, enough of that haha.

Seriously though, a big reason guys fuck up texting and come off as needy is because they give it WAY too much importance. If you make a girl feel attracted to you in person and can reel her in like that, then that's 10 times more meaningful than if you can send a few slick text messages.

I get a lot of messages from guys saying they're great at in-person communication, but suck at texting. On one hand, it's good that some of you guys are already good at talking to girls in person, but texting is nowadays usually the first step and sets off the initial vibe for dates, so you should be good at it too. An easy way to fix this is to just forget about texting and only use it the way I outlined above: to setup plans, and to keep the sexual momentum going.

A lot of guys lose sight of what they're actually trying to do when texting a girl because they freeze up and get anxious about fucking it up.

The reason you're texting this girl in the first place is to hangout with her and meet up in person so you can stick the tip in and diddle her like you've been dreaming about. You're not texting her because you want a fucking pen pal.

Fuck that.

Besides, like I mentioned earlier, generations of guys have picked up and fucked hordes of girls the old fashioned way when texting wasn't a thing, so it just goes to show that it's far more important to only use it as a fast pass to getting more dates. Think of texting as if it was just a filtering method for girls you actually ask out.

It might even be interesting to ask your grandpa how he used to get pussy without being able to text his side hoes. Actually, fuck it let's do it.

Homework: go out and ask your dad or grandpa how he used to fuck girls without using a phone

Look at that, you'll be strengthening your family relationships and learning how to fuck more girls at the same time. You'll only kill two birds with one stone like this when watching your boy,

Based Zeus.

In summary:

- Use texting as a tool

- Use it to setup dates

- Use it to build and maintain momentum

- And to minimize her perceived risk of meeting up in person

And that's it. BE SURE to keep these in mind moving forward because it's vital to succeeding with the more advanced parts of the course.

And those advance parts of the course are where it really gets interesting.

So I hope you're ready.

CHAPTER 2

What to Do When You Get Her Number

If you've ever been on the Internet or watched ANY movie, then I'm sure you've heard the rule that you're supposed to wait at least 3 days before texting a girl after getting her number.

Listen to me closely, THIS IS THE ABSOLUTE WORST ADVICE EVER.

Why would you ever wait that fucking long just send a girl a text? Are you fucking serious?

That's ridiculous.

Here's what happens if you wait 3 days:

First off, she's gonna totally forget giving you her number within 24 hours of you meeting her. Secondly, all the momentum and interest you built with her is going to dissipate within the first 48 hours, and lastly, within 72 hours she's already totally forgotten about you and will probably never think of you again.

So now let me ask you, do you REALLY want to wait 3 fucking days to text a girl? Fuck no.

You should text her RIGHT after you get her number or a few hours later. This way, all the interest she has in you, is maintained and built up even more. This also prevents her from forgetting about you and flaking on your messages. Also, she probably doesn't expect you to text her right away, so it will make you stand out and even more appealing.

If you text a girl after 3 days when all of her interest is lost, then you've successfully given her no incentive to text you back. Think about it from her perspective, why would you text this guy who took so long to hit you up and whom you're no longer interested in? It makes no sense and that's why you should do it immediately to execute on that interest.

So you've got her number and now you know that you need to text her immediately but what do you even say?

Oh shit you're expecting me to tell you that right? My bad.

When first texting her, you gotta send her something funny, something playful, and something that'll make her interested in continuing the conversation.

I prefer to tease her about something you guys talked about in person or text her saying something flirty like, "Hey it's Zeus, your soulmate. We met earlier remember?" Throw a quick emoji in there and you'll be slam dunking in that pussy in no time baby.

I'll go way more in-depth on the best opening lines and teasing but that's just a quick example of what your first text to her should be.

From there you should have a conversation with her that emphasizes building on the existing momentum and interest established when you first met her. But don't forget - you should still keep it light and playful. So if you built her interest by being really funny in person, then you should be funny over text and double down on that because it's what pushed her to give you her number in the first place.

Similarly, if you were really sarcastic and witty in person then you should replicate that in the texts you sent her as well.

Essentially what you're doing with the text conversation is showing her the reason she gave you her number in the first place, and showing her why she should be EVEN more interested in you.

In this initial conversation you should DEFINITELY be teasing her about the fact that you guys are going to hangout and depending on how well the conversation goes, you can even try planning a date right there on the spot.

I've typically found it best to go in and ask for the date during the 2nd, 3rd, or 4th text conversation. Any more than 4 conversations and she'll lose interest. The reason I sometimes refrain from asking the first time is because she may feel like she doesn't know you well enough to feel comfortable and safe with you so she'll reject the offer even if she is into you, and it'll just slow down your momentum.

Now I know I'm a god and I'm teaching you this stuff in order for you guys to follow it and be successful with it BUT, I don't want you to think these are hard and fast rules that are set in stone. Maybe the girl is really open and down to hangout so in that case it would be appropriate to ask right there during the first text convo, it really just depends. Every situation is different and hey some girls like to move fast too, so you should try to figure out yourself what kind of person she is and act accordingly.

A big part of texting and dating in general is being confident in the value and fun you can provide the girl and using that as your guiding force. Besides, you should relax and feel free to do what you think is best in situations anyways since dating and texting a girl is supposed to be something fun so you shouldn't stress yourself out about it.

If you're ever stuck in a situation, just think back to the advice I've given you, take into account what you know about the girl and your relationship so far, and most of all take a fucking chill pill and just be confident because trust me, being confident will make all of your interactions with women 10 times better, easier and it will be natural.

The Best Openers

The main thing you need to keep in mind when sending a text message to a girl is that you're sending a text in order to elicit some sort of response.

So when sending text messages, you wanna send shit that stands out and makes you WAY different than all the other guys hitting up this one hot girl you're talking to. You want to make her feel some emotions when she's texting you.

It's pointless to be just her texting buddy she replies to when she doesn't have anything to do.

Think of it like this, if you're a decently hot girl you most likely have at least 3 or 4 guys hitting you up on a daily basis. Being in this position not only puts the girl in a position of power but it also puts her in a position wherein she sees massive amounts of volume in terms of the messages that guys send her.

So with all the texts the girl you like probably gets regularly, and all the texts she's seen, you really think texting her some shit like "hey what's up?" is gonna get you a response and make her

wanna sleep with you? FUCK NO.

Your opening messages need to signal that you're not only confident, but that you're in a position of power and that you have equal amounts of girls hitting you up. This is what will really make her chase you and want to text you first.

So when sending an opening message, you should be thinking to yourself, how can I make this more unique? And from there you can start making your messages more and more unique until it just becomes second nature and you become a baller who ONLY thinks of unique messages to send. Remember, the goal isn't to try and memorize all these tools and tricks and always have them in your head to use, they are a GUIDE meant to show you what works until you become a lady-killer, badass who does them instinctively without even needing to think twice.

You probably have those fancy one-liners that make the girls drip somewhere in your head. You just need to learn how to express it through text.

Alright so now that we got that out the way, you ready to see all THE best opening lines that I personally use myself? Ready? OK here they are.

Hahah oh shit I crack myself up. Ok ok, I'm done fucking with you guys now.

One of my easy opening lines I like to use is "Your evening entertainment has arrived". This is a good one because you can substitute evening with morning or afternoon or whatever time of day it is if you're from another planet and have more than 3 times of day.

This is a perfect opener because it sets a fun tone for the rest of the conversation and signals your confidence and power because only a confident guy would make a claim like that for his first text to a girl so I really like this line.

Another line I like to use is "I'm here to initiate the beginning of our romantic love story that'll end with tragedy." This is a really sarcastic way to open but it's also good because it sets the tone of the conversation to be talking about you and her and your supposed love story. I actually used this in a conversation with a girl recently, here's the screenshot.

But more importantly, it sets the tone for that intimate and personal communication. That "Me,

You" communication is established with a text like this and that "Me,

You" communication is what you wanna establish in your interactions with women every time you talk to them. It makes the conversation inherently sexual and makes it easier to set up and deliver flirty and sexual banter.

I actually used this line in a conversation with a girl recently, here's the screenshot. As you can see, it established the conversation as being one about us and our fake love story, but it created a really easy setup to ask her to hangout in a slick, yet smooth way.

And as I'm sure you can guess, it ended in me taking her to pound town baby.

Another really good way to open a text conversation with the girl is to make a callback to something you talked about in person or in a previous conversation.

So for example, if you guys previously talked about a TV show or a really funny youtuber you both love to watch, then you can shoot her a text about it. Something like "Did you see what just happened last episode?" or something to that effect.

You can also use callback humor to tease her or make a joke about something you guys mentioned in the past. I'll break this down in my teasing and flirting videos later in the course but it's really similar to the example I just gave previously about mentioning a TV show or something but in this case, it'd be used for something more personal between you two.

A really dope thing I like to do is text myself from the girl's phone when we first exchange numbers and text something like "It was so great meeting you, I now know what it feels like to meet the love of my life." This way you can respond to it something flirty and have the conversation started for you in the frame that you want to establish for the relationship between the two of you.

Lastly, it's worth mentioning that you shouldn't be afraid to take risks with the text messages you send. Especially the texts you're sending to initiate a conversation because at the end of the day, the more unique it is, the more likely she is to respond.

This brings me to the homework for today's video.

Go out and send a girl you're talking to an opening text that is riskier than you would normally send, and see how the results differ from the regular bullshit you usually text a girl.

And don't pussy out on this one, literally pull your phone out right now and send it, no excuses. I'll be watching.

How to Use Emojis to Build Sexual Tension

I actually did a whole video on my channel about using emojis when texting a girl but that was a while ago and since then, I've found WAY better methods and tactics for using emojis with girls. And I'm even gonna show you my emoji keyboard so you know which ones are the best to use when texting girls.

You ready? Of course you're fucking ready, you're in here watching the video so let's not bullshit.

Before I break down how to use them and what the best emojis are, I'm gonna cover some of the more basic shit.

So here's a list of Don'ts, basically shit for you to

NOT do.

Don't use too many emojis.

Don't use emojis more than she uses emojis.

Don't use pussy ass emojis.

Don't use emojis to express real emotions.

HOW TO TEXT A GIRL (GODLY TEXTING)

Oh my god. This is some shit that parents do.

They get angry at you and then they send you the angry emoji, like how the fuck is anyone supposed to take you seriously if you're using fucking emojis to express REAL emotions.

Okay, okay rant over.

Oh fuck wait don't even get me started on that fucking emoji movie HOLY SHIT.

Alright now that we got that out the way let's break this down.

Right now, I'm gonna show you MY emoji keyboard, so you can get a feel of what emojis

I use most when texting girls. This way you can also see which emojis are the best to use.

Literally, just steal the ones I use and have on screen now so you can use them in your own text conversations with girls and you'll start noticing immediate differences in how girls talk to you.

Now that I showed you which emojis I use, here's how you want to use these emojis.

Basically you want to use emojis to lighten the mood of the conversation and start to tease the sexual tension between you guys.

HOW TO TEXT A GIRL (GODLY TEXTING)

Emojis are useful because they allow you to get away with saying a lot more than you could without them. They make the conversation less serious and are a really good way to get your point across over text.

Anytime you text someone it's easy for them to misinterpret what you're saying but with emojis it's a lot easier to drive your point home while also setting a flirty vibe.

There are a few ways you can use emojis to make a girl more into you over text.

The first way is to use what I call, Irony Emojis.

Basically, using a bunch of emojis in a really sarcastic and cringey way so that the girl knows you're kidding. The point of doing this is to tease something sexual or flirty while also keeping it fun and entertaining.

Here's an example of a girl actually using this trick on me. As you can see, she's using emojis ironically to tease me during our conversation.

You can do this same exact thing to girls when texting them in order to keep it light and keep that teasing, back and forth vibe going.

I use this a ton because I tend to have a sarcastic sense of humor already so it fits right in with my text conversations. However, this is a really good way to set up that teasing vibe that's crucial to any conversation with a girl.

The second way is to use emojis for comedic effect.

So for example, you use emojis to poke fun at the girl when teasing her or you use them to simply make a joke.

For example, anytime I make a joke or say something that a girl doesn't understand, I'll send a bunch of airplane emojis and follow it by saying "That one went right over your head".

Haha see what I did there? I'm laughing just thinking about it!

Another trick I like to use is to write out what the girl is saying in emojis to make fun of it.

So if she says she was out walking her dog, I'll use the girl walking emoji, the dog emoji, and then just throw the shit emoji in there to make it funny. I'll add a witty comment afterwards and boom, you've made your conversation 10x more interesting than all the other guys she texts.

Lastly, I'll use emojis when I'm teasing the girl or when I say something flirty so it signals those sexual undertones.

For this, the wink emoji, the smirk emoji, and the eye emojis are the best ones to use.

And if you wanna know what emojis I use most when texting girls well here's a screenshot of all the emojis I use when talking to girls.

And that's it.

In summary:

- Avoid using emojis like a bitch

- Use the Irony Emojis

- Use emojis for comedic effect

- And use emojis when teasing a girl

And don't think I forgot to assign you homework for this one so here it is.

I want you to go out and try using the Irony

Emojis in one of your text conversations to see how well it works and you can get used to applying it in your interactions.

Zeus out.

Text, Tease, and Takeoff: In-Depth

If someone put a gun to my head and told me to teach them the number one texting tip, I would have to teach them the T.T.T. method and then strike them with lightning for putting a gun to my head, but that's beside the point. T.T.T. stands for Text, Tease, and Takeoff and it's how you should frame all of your conversations with girls over text, snapchat, or any other online messaging.

The first part of T.T.T. is something I already covered in depth when I talked about the best openers to start a text conversation. Basically don't start a text conversation with "hi", "hey", "what's up", "wyd", "hey cutie", or any of those generic ass lines I KNOW some of you guys have used before. If you're subscribed to Based

Zeus then it's time to cut that shit out because Basedlympians are much more interesting than that 6th grade shit. Like I've always said, if the shit you're texting her wouldn't work on you if you were a girl, then DON'T FUCKING SEND IT.

The Teasing part of T.T.T. is the hardest and it's where I see most guys struggle. Usually when you text a girl you probably ask her what she's doing, how her day was, what she ate, what TV show she's watching, and a lot of other dumb shit like that. The common theme among this nonsense a lot of guys text girls is that there's no real incentive to respond to text messages like this. Her parents probably already asked her all of those dumb questions. She doesn't need more of those conversations. Instead of saying "hey what's up" open with something that you guys talked about before like a cafe you both wanted to go to, then you could say something like "guess where I'm eating" and then send her a pic of the food or the place or whatever. You get the idea. If one guy sends the girl the bullshit "hey what's up" and another guy opens with "bet you're really jealous I'm eating here right now" and sends a pic of a place they talked about, who do you think she's going to want to respond to more? Exactly. Be that guy

Mentioning stuff you guys have talked about before to open the conversation is also better because it allows for you to start teasing her right off the bat and allows for a more flirtatious conversation. Usually when you approach a girl for the first time, your opening line doesn't matter a whole lot, but when texting, it matters a whole lot more because it sets the tone for the entire conversation. Also, this way if some time elapses between messages it'll also help maintain the teasing and flirting aspect since how you open a conversation through text usually translates into how the rest of the messages will follow. For example, texting a girl the normal bullshit "hey," just says to her that you want to talk to her because you're into her and are trying to make her into you. But opening with a sarcastic or funny comment about something you guys previously discussed is much more subtle and makes her think you probably thought of it and it reminded you of her so you texted her since it's something you've talked about before. This makes you seem much less desperate and

10x more interesting.

Besides, are you really THAT boring that you can't come up with something better to say than "hey what's up?" If you're a Basedlympian, that means you're a badass and actually have a personality, unlike most guys, so show it.

Now, when it comes to the third T which stands for Takeoff in case you got lost in all this godly advice I've been giving, you want to make sure you're always letting the conversation finish organically. For example, if you think the conversation is coming to a natural end, then it probably is so you should go ahead and stop replying to her. Remember to always keep in mind that the ultimate goal with texting is to actually go out with the girl in person. For this reason, you should use texting to achieve that goal and use it to set up plans, occasionally tease/flirt with her, and keep momentum going.

You don't want to be that annoying guy that texts her all day, every day because then she'll just see you as someone to talk to when she's super bored and has nothing better to do which in case you didn't know, is the opposite of what you want to become.

Another way to end the conversation is to leave at a high point, for example when you guys are flirting heavily and there's a lot of sexual tension going on. This way, you leave her wanting more and she'll be eager to talk to you next time you see her or text her. If you're really looking to build her interest, you can even disappear in the middle of a really flirty conversation and do a 1-1.5 day pull away. But this isn't something you want to do often because it can make her get annoyed with you and then she'll start doing the same to you, so use this combination sparingly.

I'll breakdown the pull away in-depth and give you examples of the pull away structure I personally use, in order to build a girl's interest in a later video.

And that's it.

In summary:

• Use the openers I've talked about to open up the text conversation

• Tease the girl about something you guys have talked about in the past

• And takeoff at the conversation's natural end or at a high point to leave her wanting more

How to Tease a Girl over Text

I get asked this question all the time, "Zeus how do you tease a girl over text?"

Well lucky for you, I'm gonna break this down and show you.

The main method I personally use to tease a girl is something I like to call Magnifying. Magnifying is also known as playful misinterpretation which is basically where you stretch or exaggerate whatever she says into something totally different.

So for example, if a girl says she likes to go to the gym. You can say something like "Oh wow that's dope, I had no idea you were a nationally recognized bodybuilder who can benchpress my bodyweight."

It's totally out of the blue and completely ridiculous but at its core, that's what teasing is all about. Taking the ordinary things a girl says, and stretching it into something really ridiculous that establishes a playful vibe.

You want to establish this playful vibe with a girl because it's a precursor and more importantly, a preliminary requirement for establishing a sexual vibe with her. You also want to make her feel like you are somebody who's fun to hang out with and who is able to make her laugh throughout the day.

Another way you can tease a girl is to playfully make fun of something she's doing. So for example, I was texting this girl and she told me that she went out with her friends to get one of those fruit bowls with yogurt and shit and then she sent me a pic of it. I then teased her by saying "That looked like a really healthy snack until you drowned it in chocolate. Didn't know chocolate could be so healthy!"

You see what I did there, I took something small that she did without realizing and then just teased her about it. Really simple shit like that you can turn into an opportunity to tease the girl.

If a girl says she likes to do yoga, you can tease her about being a hippie who's gonna try and read your spiritual energy.

Basically magnify whatever it is she says into something that's funny, ridiculous, and most importantly of all, playful. Once you get the hang of it, it will all be coming naturally and you won't even have to try to look for things to tease her about.

This playful vibe will show that you're a fun guy to be around whose not afraid to push the boundaries and doesn't put her on a pedestal.

Because if you did, you'd be too afraid to tease her which you're not. But you should learn to recognize what is probably not the best idea to be teasing the girl about. If you start making fun of her about something she actually really cares about, it might hit her too deep and be counterproductive.

Additionally, teasing a girl like this is an easy way to signal your confidence to her because you're confident and not afraid to push her buttons and ruffle her feathers, and hopefully a little bit more than that haha.

It also signals abundance because if you're not afraid to potentially lose her, it means that you have an abundance of other bitches to hit up, an abundance of happiness in your life, and an abundance of cool shit in your life.

Now you obviously don't wanna say some shit like "Wow you're eating for the 4th time today, you really are a fat fucking bitch." That's definitely

NOT teasing. But if you take something she says and magnify it like I described, you'll be well on your way to creating that playful vibe, and more importantly, that sexual vibe which I KNOW you horny motherfuckers are trying to go for.

How to Flirt Like a God

Flirting with a girl over text. How to do it. Well I'm gonna show you right motherfuckin now. You ready? Ok good.

First of all the most important thing you need to understand when flirting with a girl over text is what's known in the pickup community as

"Me, You" communication or man to woman communication. A lot of pickup artists have a whole fucking science and bible based around this man to woman or "Me, You" communication which is totally unnecessary.

Basically, all you need to know is that "Me, You" communication is a form of flirting that involves centering the conversation around you and her.

When you focus the conversation on you and her it almost immediately makes the context of the conversation flirtatious AND it makes it really easy for you to flirt with her because the context of the conversation is about well you and her, obviously. This kind of flirting also feels more genuine and personal, so it's very effective.

When a conversation is centered around a man and a woman and you contextualize things as

"Me, you", it's the perfect setup for flirtatious comments and flirty banter.

For example, I matched with a girl on Tinder that I actually know in real life and have talked to before. So I screenshotted that we matched on Tinder and texted her the picture of it and used it as a way to flirt with by joking that her and I matched on Tinder and that it would be the start of our romantic love story. Boom, right there I established the "Me, you" communication and as you can see, the rest of the conversation is flirtatious as fuck and centered around me and her.

The fact that it was centered around me and her also made it really easy for me to continue flirting with her and saying things like you and I need to go on a romantic date, you and I blah blah, you get the point I'm making.

I'll show you another example of this in a text conversation I had with a different girl. You'll see that the whole conversation is basically just me finding creative ways of centering it around her and I, and from there I'm just making flirty and witty comebacks. A lot of guys would love to know how to be smoother, and wittier, in conversation with a girl, and establishing this type of communication is exactly how you do it.

It makes being flirtatious and sexual with a girl, effortless because the inherent nature of this type of communication is flirty.

If you're still having trouble figuring out how to flirt with a girl OR how to establish this sort of communication just think of it like this.

When you're in the middle of a text conversation with a girl, think to yourself, "How can I frame this as a 'Me, You' conversation?"

Or even easier than that, you could also just try using the words, "me" and "you" in the conversation and from there it'll turn the conversation in the direction you want it to go.

Literally just adding in the word "you", makes these interactions more flirtatious and makes it way easier to setup flirty and sexual comments.

The most important thing you want to accomplish with this type of communication is establishing the sexual undertones. One way you can do it is to outright acknowledge it. This is a risky move, but if done correctly, you can actually accomplish a lot and it'll make your interactions with the girl way more sexual. Here's an example of how I did it by simply using the words "you" and "I" in the very beginning of the interaction.

In fact, you'll notice that those two words are used in almost every text I send to a girl, and it makes the conversations way more flirtatious and sexual. It also established some kind of connection, because you are referring to both of you as "us" and gives it a vibe as if you were a unit.

And that's actually going to be your homework assignment for today's video:

Go out and try using these words in conversations with at least 3 girls. Doesn't matter if the girl is ugly or if it's over Tinder or Bumble. Just practice using this type of communication with as many girls as possible, so you can become really good at it until it becomes natural and effortless.

You can also apply this to in person interactions with girls as well. Basically just establish that

"Me, you" communication and use it to frame the conversation in a flirtatious way and you'll be on your way. This technique is probably going to be even more useful for in-person interactions, because when you communicate with a girl directly, you can put here even more into that "us" zone.

Bonus tip: combine the "Me, you" communication with the magnifying tactic I showed you in the how to tease a girl over text video and you'll be able to flirt with girls and establish that sexual vibe over text instantly.

Yeah I know, it's fucking awesome. You're welcome.

Zeus out.

CHAPTER 3

Advanced Techniques from the Gods

What to Do When She Doesn't Reply

So you're texting the girl you're into, and mid conversation when things were seemingly going fine, she disappears on you and leaves you with no response.

HOW TO TEXT A GIRL (GODLY TEXTING)

Trust me I get it. Girls used to leave me on read

ALL the time, for seemingly no reason.

But what I've found is this, the way you react to her ghosting you is EXTREMELY important. This is super simple and guys overthink this situation so much.

It's not that complicated. You basically have two options when a girl ghosts you:

1. You can complain about it to her and ask her why she's not responding to you

2. You can just ignore it and act like nothing happened.

Now I don't know about you but option 1 is THE absolute worst thing you can do. It shows her that you're needy, not confident, and don't have interesting shit going on because if you did then you wouldn't be sitting around worried about whether or not she responded to you.

Option 1 accomplishes nothing because even if she does tell you why she didn't respond, what are you gonna do then? It doesn't change the fact that she didn't respond to you, all it does is make you look like a little bitch.

Plus, a lot of times a girl will forget to respond for a while and then she'll hit you back up a few hours later, or the next day. So most of the time, it makes the most sense to just ignore it and act like she just forgot.

Another question I get a lot is, "Zeus what do I do if she stops responding to my text but sends me a snap later on?"

Well, here's your answer.

If she she sends you a snapchat a little while later instead of responding to you then just assume that's the same as her responding to you.

Like I said, option 2 is the best way to react because it shows her that you're still a guy of status.

She didn't respond to one of your messages, so what? You shouldn't let it hurt your confidence because then that would only mean that she's the one in control of the relationship which is exactly what you DON'T want.

If a girl doesn't respond, and I still feel like talking to her, sometimes I'll just say fuck it and send her another text talking about something totally different that we've talked about before.

You don't want to overthink this, if a guy friend of yours didn't respond to your last text, does that mean he doesn't wanna be friends with you anymore? FUCK No. It just means he didn't think your text warranted a response, or he got busy, or he just forgot, who fucking knows.

Just act like nothing and text her again the next day if you feel like it.

Too many guys use texting as a way to make them either confident or insecure in the relationship, and this is why guys freak out so much when a girl doesn't reply.

The next time a girl doesn't respond to your text, just pause, take a deep breath, stop being a little bitch, and just do what you were gonna do anyways.

It's that simple.

And that's it.

In summary:

- Act like nothing happened and don't acknowledge it

- Send her another text if you have another topic of conversation to start

- Or just wait till the next day and start a new conversation as if nothing happened

How to Keep the Conversation Going

So you've been going through the course, learning the basics, and now you have a good foundation for texting girls.

You know what to say, you know what to avoid, and you can start conversations with girls pretty easily.

But keeping the conversation going for longer periods of time, and keeping it interesting, is totally different and therefore, requires a different approach.

In this video, I'm gonna break down EXACTLY how to not only keep conversations going but

ALSO make sure they keep the girl interested and invested in the conversation, the entire time.

#1 Use the Magnifying Method.

I talked about magnifying in my earlier video on

How to Tease a Girl Over Text.

Basically, magnifying is using playful misinterpretation to tease and flirt with a girl.

This is basically where you stretch or exaggerate whatever she says into something totally different for the sake of making the conversation fun and light.

I break this down entirely in that video, so if you didn't watch that, then go check that out first.

Magnifying is a powerful and easy method for keeping the conversation going because all it requires you to do is, stretch whatever she says into a joke.

Right there, you've started an entirely new conversation that's also fun and interesting.

Not to mention, it also sets up the perfect vibe for building sexual tension.

#2 Don't always keep the conversation going.

This sounds counterintuitive but it's JUST as important as any other conversational tactic or

trick.t

Conversations have a natural end, once a conversation reaches that natural end, DON'T

FORCE IT.

Forcing a conversation to continue after it's natural end will make for a boring and dull conversation anyways so it's better to let it end.

Additionally, if you have a forced conversation with a girl, she's more likely to get bored and just stop responding. Not to mention, it'll also make her think that YOU are boring which is the exact opposite of what you want her to think.

You want her to think, you're that cool, interesting guy who she actually likes and wants to talk to.

#3 Remove your confidence from the equation.

I've answered thousands of guys DMs, messages, and comments, all relating to texting and one thing I noticed over and over again was that SO many guys attach their confidence to their text conversation.

HOW TO TEXT A GIRL (GODLY TEXTING)

For example, you're texting a girl, you guys are flirting back and forth, she's adding a lot to the conversation as well and seems SUPER down, and then suddenly, out of nowhere, she stops responding.

Leaving you feeling like an idiot and wondering what you did wrong.

This is a bad reaction, and more importantly it's a bad habit that so many guys have.

They attach their confidence and self-worth in the relationship to their text conversations.

You have to be unreactive and willing to accept the fact that sometimes a girl isn't gonna hit you back. It's part of the game. I've had girls stop responding to my texts, just for them to text ME first and ask me to hangout.

Your confidence should not be hurt just because a girl didn't respond to you. Do you even hear how stupid that sounds?

Could you imagine me, Based Zeus, getting hurt and upset just because ONE girl didn't answer one of my texts? FUCK NO.

I'm still a god, regardless if she left me on read or not.

A lot of guys, get validation and feel better about themselves when the girl responds to them, and if the girl doesn't respond, they feel like shit.

This isn't true confidence, this is seeking approval from girls which is the total opposite.

For this reason, a lot of texting boils down to a confidence problem, not an actual problem with your text game. If you're not confident, your text game is gonna show it, and you're gonna fuck things up.

But if you are confident, and you signal your confidence to girls like I outlined in the first module, then your text game will be significantly better and you'll achieve more results.

Basically, don't keep the conversation going for the sake of keeping it going. Keep it going, in order to build more flirtiness and momentum in the relationship, or if you want to ask her to hangout.

However, DON'T keep it going just because texting her all day every day, makes you feel good and makes you think she's still into you.

Because trust me, plenty of girls will text guys they're not into just out of boredom so don't fall into this trap.

Go into the conversation knowing what you want to achieve, and once you do it and the conversation comes to a natural end, then leave it at that.

And that's it.

In summary:

• Use the magnifying method

• Don't always keep the convo going

• And remove your confidence from the equation

Your homework for today's video: is to go out and use the magnifying method in a text conversation to make it more interesting and keep it going for just a little while longer.

You can use this on Tinder, in the DMs, or with one of the girls you've been texting while taking this course.

Try it out, and be sure to comment and let me know how much pussy you get.

The Pull away: In-Depth

Disclaimer, I have a full video on this topic on my channel that I personally consider to be one of my best videos to date. You should watch that video as well.

As you guys know I'm very against bullshit "games" and "tactics" and more about simply taking action, but this method is perhaps one of the most important ones for any guy to learn in order to increase his success with women.

When I first discovered this back in high school, it literally blew my mind and I thought I was going to become the next Hugh Hefner with the amount of girls it got me. This godly texting method is known as "The Pull away" and it comes straight from Mount Olympus.

My standard routine for doing a pull away is to text a girl for anywhere between 2-4 days in a row (I usually text her for 2.5-3 days) followed by a 1-2 day pull away where I totally go off the radar and don't talk to the girl at all. This includes not replying to any texts she sends to you.

Zeus's Pull away brought to you in part by your need to have sex with beautiful women haha.

My pull away is usually 2-3 days of texting plus 1-1.5 days (sometimes 2 days) without talking to the girl at all.

You may be wondering how NOT texting a girl can actually make her more interested in you, but it's actually quite simple. You've been texting her consistently for a few days and then all of a sudden you don't text her at all for a day or two and don't respond to any of her messages. Now, she's forced to think "Why isn't he answering?

Why hasn't he texted me all day? I wonder what he's doing that he's not talking to me, wouldn't he have mentioned it? Did I say something wrong last time we talked? Does he not like me anymore? Is he still into me? Does he still want to hangout this weekend?" As you can see, breaking the rhythm like this forces her to think about you A LOT MORE than she previously was and it forces her to think of you as a guy who has more interesting shit to do than text her all day every day even if you're actually nerdy guy who's intentionally ignoring her because you read my advice.

Girls like guys who have a lot of things going on in their life and this makes you seem like one of those productive and cool guys, even if you aren't. This makes you seem a lot more unpredictable and spontaneous which keeps girls interested WAY more than being like most guys who are too predictable and available all the time. Guys who aren't always available are inherently more attractive to girls because it makes them seem more desirable. And when you do actually give her attention, she'll be all over you because she doesn't know when she'll be able to talk to you again. It's like going on a really expensive vacation to an exotic place, you're going to take advantage of it and soak it up as much as you can while you're there because you don't know if/when you'll be back there again.

The pull away is also a really good way of signaling abundance because she knows you're not chasing her around constantly hitting her up and thinking about her if you can go sometime without hitting her up at all. It also peaks her curiosity and makes you seem a lot more mysterious. And in case you didn't know, curiosity and mystery are very similar if not the same exact thing as attraction. When you're wondering about who someone else, what they do, and why they behave the way they do, it makes you attracted to them and their life. So creating curiosity and mystery is a really good way of making women WAY more attracted to you.

I've had a ton of guys message me after using the pull away and telling me that they couldn't believe how well it worked and how much of a difference it's made in their texting game.

It also makes her question how much you like her - since she'd expect you to be talking to her if you were into her. This is also good for you because then she'll be more upfront about being interested in you when you talk to her again since she'll be worried that you're losing interest in her and may potentially lose you.

A really good tactic I like to use is to ask the girl to hangout right when I come back from doing

a pull away because as soon as she hears from me again is when she's most interested and at a high point so it makes it easy for her to commit to hanging out with me since this is when her interest is peaked.

I'll go more in depth in a later video on how to get her to hangout and increase her chances of saying yes but I don't want this video to drag on and go on a tangent.

So in summary:

My pull away is between 2-3 days of texting back and forth followed by a 1 to 1 and a half day

Pull away. This structure is what's gotten me the most amount of girls.

Try it out.

How to Know if She Likes You over Text

You've been texting the girl you like for a while but you're STILL not sure if she likes you too. Or you think she's into you but you're not exactly sure how into you she is.

This right here is a BAD position to be in. When put in a position like this, most guys lose a lot of confidence in the situation because they feel as though they need to make the girl like them.

This video right here is probably one of THE most important videos in this course. So strap yourself in and get ready to experience the godliness.

The first thing you need to understand is this: If a girl doesn't like you then there is only one thing for you to do. MOVE THE FUCK ON.

Seriously, I mean that. This is a huge problem for guys. Guys will either get outright rejected or a really strong hint from a girl that she's not into them and then STILL try pursuing the girl.

Dude, if a girl rejects you or you find out she doesn't like you then the only thing left for you to do is to move on. Yes, it fucking sucks but I mean, how bad does it really suck?

There are literally 3 billion more girls out there for you to go after and more likely than not, you're a younger guy with your whole life ahead of you and dozens of girls to meet and be with.

If you're still in high school or college, I can guarantee you that the girl you're all in love with now, will be totally irrelevant to your life within a few months, and within a year or two, you will have completely forgotten about her!

Use this knowledge and take dating for what it is. A fun experience to enjoy in the present, not added stress. Knowing this is empowering and gives you the freedom to not be too emotional over a negative experience with a girl.

This mindset is absolutely CRUCIAL to understand when it comes to texting girls. So it's your job to keep that in mind.

Now that you're in the right mindset and not too attached to a girl before you even know her, it's time to learn.

So the easiest way for you to find out if a girl likes you is to employ what I call "The Hangout

Test."

The hangout test is a tactic I've taught on my channel in the past but I'll give you a quick breakdown of what it is to refresh your memory

AND I'm even gonna give you some updated tips on it that I've learned recently.

Basically, if you've been texting a girl for a while, all you do is ask the girl to hangout over text.

That's it!

If she responds and says yes, then she likes you enough to invest the time in meeting up and hanging out with you so you have your answer.

If she responds and says no and gives you an excuse then it's not likely that she's into you.

There are a few caveats to think about if she says no though, if she says no and gives you a

REALLY legit-ass excuse then you can assume that she's actually busy.

BUT, if she gives you a really legit excuse and doesn't suggest another time to hangout with you then you can assume she's not into you.

Most of the time if a girl isn't interested in hanging with you, she'll give a lame ass excuse and not offer another time for you guys to hangout.

BUT if she is into you, she might still say no if she has an actual excuse and she'll offer another time for you guys to hangout. In this case, this means she's actually into you and WANTS to hangout.

Now if she rejects your offer and doesn't offer another time to hangout then I'll repeat the process to see if she says yes the second time around.

If she rejects your offer to hangout two to three times and doesn't offer an alternate time, then it's safe to assume she doesn't want to hangout with you and you should move on from her to avoid wasting anymore time.

The second way to see if she's into you is to see how flirty she is with you in your text conversations and more importantly, see how she responds to your flirty and sexual comments.

A girl who's not into you won't respond to flirty texts and she sure as hell won't reciprocate

flirtiness.

So a really easy way to test out her level of interest is to make a flirty comment to her and see how she responds. A really easy line you can use on her when she teases you or says almost anything is "Stop flirting with me" or "Are you flirting with me?"

Depending on how she responds to that line, you'll be able to gauge her level of interest in you. I even recommend using this line in person on the girl because it's an easy way to see her response to the idea of flirting with you and it'll give a good idea of where she's at in the relationship.

There are also a few questions you should consider asking yourself, I call this the Question

Test.

Here are the questions you should ask.

When you tease or mention the idea of you guys hanging out do her texts indicate that she's interested in hanging out with you?

Does she tease at the idea of you guys hanging out?

Does she text you first? Or are you the one texting her first?

If she texts you first then that's a fairly good indicator of her interest in you and you should execute on that interest fast and hang out with her in person.

If she doesn't react well to the idea of you guys hanging out then it's an indication that she probably doesn't feel comfortable enough with you to hangout yet. So that means you need to make her feel more comfortable and show her that you're a cool, normal guy.

Once you reflect on these questions, test her level of flirtiness, and use the hangout test, you'll have a way better understanding of how much the girl you're texting likes you, and how to move forward from there.

So your homework for today's video is to apply the hangout test and the question text to conversations you're having with girls and seeing how much they're interested in you. If they're not interested in you, then it's time to evaluate the convos you've been having with girls and seeing what you need to fix.

How to Make Her Text You First

Alright guys, it's time, it's finally time. You're gonna learn how to get these bitches to start texting you first!

Crack open those notebooks because I'm gonna show you exactly what it takes to make a girl text you first. You ready? Fuck yeah you are,

I know you got a boner just thinking about this topic haha.

Let's do it.

Approach #1: Create Scarcity.

I briefly went over this in one of my emails to you but I'll give you an even deeper breakdown of it before I get into the other approaches.

Basically, you have to show her that you're a guy of high status. A guy whose high status is a guy who clearly has an abundance of girls, and more importantly, good shit going on in his life.

You need her to believe that you're a high status guy so this way she understands that you're a man of abundance and it creates the most important thing necessary to kick start a romantic relationship. That thing is scarcity.

If a girl sees that you have a ton of good shit going for you, then she knows that she needs to compete for your attention because you have so much shit going on that your time and attention are both scarce. So she'll do everything in her power to get your attention and latch onto you when she does have your attention.

And what's a really easy way for her to get your attention? Yup, that's right, sending YOU a text message. She knows that you have shit going for you and that if she doesn't hit you up, then the scarce amount of interest you have in her might fade and she'll lose her chance.

The more scarce a resource is, the morevaluable it becomes.

Scarcity creates urgency. And urgency creates action.

So it's imperative that you always carry yourself like the high status guy you are and make sure you signal to girls that you're high status. The easiest way of doing this is to follow the advice

I gave in my "Signal Your Confidence" lesson because it shows you step-by-step how to make sure girls know that you're a confident badass like me. I HIGHLY recommend you rewatch that video after watching this one.

Approach #2: Establish a cadence with the girl aka a rhythm.

Let's say you're texting a girl or snapchatting her pretty regularly for a few days. Then all of a sudden she doesn't hit you up like she

HOW TO TEXT A GIRL (GODLY TEXTING)

normally does.

You're gonna think to yourself "Wow that's weird she hasn't texted me yet like she does every morning."

That's because you've established a routine wherein you were talking to her every day for a few days and then she suddenly disappeared.

So to get BACK to your routine, you're gonna hit her up first because you want to keep talking to her like you normally do.

See how that works?

You basically want to create the same effect on the girls you talk to. You can do this through snapchat, instagram, or through text. I know this course is focused on texting but what you do over snapchat, instagram, and in person all play important parts in your text game and decide whether or not your text game will work.

So if you want to create a cadence with a girl, then snapchat her every day for a few days and you can text her as well. Hell, you can even send her funny memes on Instagram too if you feel like it. Basically, have her interact with you on multiple levels so that after a few days, she'll be snapping you back often and she'll even start sending you funny stuff on Instagram as well.

This way, she gets used to talking to you and gets used to your interactions, once she gets used to your interactions is when she'll feel more and more comfortable reaching out and initiating them first.

This is part of the reason why the Pull away works so well. It establishes a conversational routine and then suddenly breaks it, causing her to think about you even more once the pattern is broken. I talk about the pull away more in-depth in my pull away video so I recommend checking that out again after watching this one.

Approach #3: Instagram

You're probably thinking, huh? What the fuck?

How is my Instagram gonna make her text me first?

Well the God is about to tell you.

Remember in approach #1 how I said that being a guy who signals abundance and high status is excellent for creating scarcity, and more importantly action?

Well you can use your Instagram to do this exact thing...

Basically, if you're living an awesome life and you're a guy who clearly has abundance and high status, then all you have to do is post badass pictures and stories on your Instagram to capture that dope life you live.

And if you don't do cool shit, then START

DOING cool shit because you should be doing dope shit on your own. This way, you have an awesome life that doesn't need girls in it and they're just an added bonus. I talk about this all the time but girls should NOT be the only thing you have in your life. They're just a plus.

Having an awesome life and simply documenting it on Instagram will show the girl you like that you're living a dope life with or without her and it'll make her want to be apart of it.

And more importantly, it'll create the scarcity which will lead her to taking action.

And that's it.

In summary:

- Create scarcity

- Establish a cadence with the girl aka a rhythm

- And use your instagram to position yourself as a high status guy

And your homework for today's video is an easy one. Go out right now and do something dope that you ACTUALLY like doing and simply document it on your Instagram story. Do this enough times and you'll see the results for yourself.

Zeus out.

The Best Way to Ask Her to Hangout

When it comes to getting dates with girls, most guys have very little success. They can do well and have successful interactions with girls up until they ask her to hangout, when she inevitably rejects them or flakes at the last second.

I know how frustrating this shit can be, there wasa time where I got rejected more than FIVE times in a single month. And each of those rejections came from girls I had been actively talking to and texting.

Basically, we'd be texting for a few days and she'd be totally into me.

Then I'd bring up the topic of hanging out and the girl would be SUPER down and we'd lock in a time and place.

But then, here comes the MAJOR issue...

The day of our scheduled date would come up and the girl would flake on me. She'd give me an excuse or would cancel on me entirely out of nowhere.

This was even more frustrating than getting rejected from the beginning because at least that way I wouldn't have to waste any time talking to them for days through text just for them to reject me anyways.

However, I quickly realized the mistake I was making.

With each girl I'd ask out, I'd follow the same formula.

Step 1: I'd text them and start the conversation off by teasing them about us hanging out

Step 2: Then I'd go ahead and actually schedule the date with them for later in the week.

The first part of that formula is actually really solid because it brings up the topic of hanging out in a really natural way that doesn't come off as pushy or needy.

The second part of the formula is where the

HUGE mistake lies.

In general, most girls follow an emotional train of thought as opposed to a logical train of thought.

Making them WAY more likely to flake on you the day of your scheduled date if it's planned too far in advance.

The long stretch of time between the ask and the actual date allows them to overthink whether or not they want to hangout with you or if you're even worth hanging out with.

She may be down to hangout with you on Monday when you're talking to her and having a flirty conversation, but by the time Saturday rolls around, she may not be down anymore.

This is why when you're trying to plan a date, it's best to start off by sending a funny or flirty text to establish a good vibe with the girl.

The best way to bring up the idea of a date is to start off by teasing the girl about something you or her are talking about or doing.

Then you can plant the seeds of the hangout by teasing and making a joke about you guys doing that thing together.

So for example, if she mentions that she goes to yoga every morning, then you can tease her or make a joke about it. Then once you do that and she reciprocates the flirty vibe, you can go ahead and tease the idea of you guys doing it together.

This way it feels natural and organic, without being too forced or formal.

After you tease the idea of you guys doing it together, you can hit her with:

1. "What are you doing today?" OR

2. "What are you doing tomorrow?"

And from there, you can set up the date.

Asking her to hangout with you at a much sooner point in time makes her less likely to flake on you because she'll be in a positive emotional state towards you AND she will have less time to

Over think it and flake.

Additionally, she'll have a better idea of what her plans are in the immediate future as opposed to when you plan something out further in advance.

Think about it like this, if someone asks you on Monday what your plans are for Saturday night, how likely are you to have plans that far in advance? Chances are you don't have plans that far ahead and haven't thought about what you'll be doing.

So when you ask a girl to hangout more than

2-3 days in advance, she doesn't know what she has planned either so if something more fun comes up, of course she's gonna flake on you because she still doesn't know if you're worth the time it takes to hangout with you.

This is why asking the day before or the day of, has the highest success rate and prevents girls from flaking on you.

If you're looking to take a girl out on a 1 on 1 date then asking anywhere from 1-2 days in advance works best.

I usually, ask the day before, after I've teased her a few times about us doing something together in previous conversations.

BUT, if you're inviting a girl out to a party or a club or some sort of nightlife event that's public and includes other people, then I actually recommend bringing this up to the girl pretty far in advance.

For example, if you know you and your friends are gonna be at a party on a Friday night, I would invite her and her friends as soon as possible because you want to prevent them from making other plans. This way, when they do go to make their plans, they'll already know about the party and they'll be more likely to show up since it's been on their mind for a few days.

Now this doesn't mean you can't invite them out to a party or club the day of, it just means that it usually works better if you plan it in advance because most girls will have party plans once the weekend rolls around. If you happen to find out the day of, then it's still better to just invite the girls anyways because there's still a chance she'll have no plans and will be down.

Side note: girls are more likely to say yes if you ask them to do something that's low pressure and casual because it'll be seen as less scary and uncomfortable. This is why inviting girls out to parties, bars, clubs, and other public activities where she can bring her friends is a good idea.

This way she's more likely to come since it's a really low pressure environment and situation.

If you're asking her out on a 1 on 1 date then

I suggest doing stuff like coffee, frozen yogurt, bubble tea, hikes, and so on.

And that's it.

In summary:

• Ask the girl to hangout the day before or the day of for 1 on 1 dates

• And if you're inviting her to a public setting with other people, then invite her further in advance

• Make sure it's a low pressure date

• And make sure to seed the date by first teasing her about something then actually asking her to do it.

Zeus out.

A Final Message from the God

And just like that, you've finally made it through. I just want to say, congratulations because you've successfully made it through the entire fucking course. Do you know how much of a badass that means you are?

You've just been successfully coached by the

God of bitches, and YOU are now a certified

God at texting.

You are now a master of all the texting psychology and techniques that WILL get you laid. But just like Spiderman, you must use these powers responsibly, if not I'll come down and strike you with lightning myself.

You now have everything you need, to go out and text and fuck girls like the God you were destined to be. And there's no excuse for it not to work because I've given you all the tools you need, and this course will always be here for you to refer back to. Should you have any further questions, be sure to leave it in the comments below and I'll get back to you.

Now go out and enjoy the gift of Godly texting

I've given you, and be sure to go through all the bonus content as well, because in it, you will learn EVEN more about how to text like a

God. In the bonuses, I exposed 30 screenshots of my own successful conversations for you to steal, the 100 best opening lines for you to use whenever you need to start a convo, and the

ebook version of the course for you to refer to whenever you encounter a texting problem. I also have the two bonus Q&A videos coming out in the next few weeks, so stay tuned for that as well.

I've now given you all you need, and I just want to say again, congratulations because you took action when others wouldn't and you made the decision to better your text game, and your life.

And for that, you should be proud of yourself.

'Til next time, Zeus out.

Link of the course and videos

https://godlytexting.com/a-texting-guide

ABOUT THE AUTHOR

    This book is All about how to text a girl (to text like a god) to level up your texting game and get girls in your bed.

    This book is going to teach you how to signal your confidence via text, the power of texting, what to do when you get her number, the best opening lines, how to use emojis to build sexual tension, how to tease a girl over the text, how to flirt like a god, what to do when she doesn't reply, how to keep a conversation going, how to know if she likes you over the text, how to make her text you first, the best way to ask her to hangout and many more if you purchase this book.

    I urge you to purchase this book if you are having problem texting a girl and start living like a god because this book written directly from mountain Olympus.

Manufactured by Amazon.ca
Acheson, AB